The Hilltop

by Lucy McClymont
illustrations by Collin Fry

Harcourt Brace & Company

Orlando Atlanta Austin Boston San Francisco Chicago Dallas New York Toronto London

Mom read that health is
more fun than wealth.

2

Dad read that bread is
good for your health.

Fred read that lifting lead
helps your health.

I read that doing the hop is
good for your health. The
Pat-Your-Head Health Hop!

This is the Pat-Your-Head
Health Hop.

Pat your head once. Say "Health!"

Now pat your head and hop!
Say "Health!"
Do this five times.

8

"Health, health, health,
health, health!"
That is the Pat-Your-Head
Health Hop!

Now take a deep breath.
Take more deep breaths.
Do the Pat-Your-Head
Health Hop again!

Hop for your health!

12